The Obama Presidency

American history, Volume 16

Michael Johnson

Published by Harmony House Publishing, 2024.

THE OBAMA PRESIDENCY

First edition. April 5, 2024.

Copyright © 2024 Michael Johnson.

ISBN: 979-8224317615

Written by Michael Johnson.

Table of Contents

Chapter 1: Introduction..1

Chapter 2: The Campaign Trail 4

Chapter 3: Election Victory..7

Chapter 4: Inauguration and Early Days................................. 11

Chapter 5: Economic Crisis and Recovery............................ 15

Chapter 6: Healthcare Reform.. 18

Chapter 7: Foreign Policy Challenges...................................... 23

Chapter 8: Climate Change and Environmental Policy 28

Chapter 9: Social Justice and Civil Rights 31

Chapter 10: Immigration Reform... 36

Chapter 11: Midterm Elections and Political Challenges 40

Chapter 12: Second Term and Legacy Building...................... 44

Chapter 13: Legacy and Impact 48

Chapter 14: Post-Presidency.. 53

Chapter 15: Conclusion.. 57

"To the spirit of hope and progress that defined an era,

This book is dedicated to all those who believed in the promise of change and rallied behind Barack Obama's vision for a brighter future. From the grassroots activists to the dedicated public servants, your tireless efforts and unwavering commitment to progress shaped the Obama presidency and inspired a nation.

May the legacy of hope and resilience forged during those transformative years continue to guide us as we strive to build a more just and inclusive society.

With gratitude and admiration,

Michael Johnson"

Chapter 1: Introduction

Setting the Stage for the Obama Presidency: The State of the Nation in 2008

The year was 2008, and the United States found itself at a pivotal moment in its history. The nation was reeling from the effects of the Great Recession, which had been triggered by the subprime mortgage crisis and had led to widespread job losses, home foreclosures, and economic uncertainty. The war in Iraq, which had been ongoing for five years, was also weighing heavily on the American psyche, with thousands of troops deployed overseas and no end in sight.

Against this backdrop of economic hardship and international conflict, the American people were hungry for change. They were tired of politics as usual, tired of partisan bickering and gridlock in Washington, and they were looking for a leader who could offer them hope for a brighter future.

Introducing Barack Obama: His Background, Rise in Politics, and Campaign Promises of Hope and Change

Born on August 4, 1961, in Honolulu, Hawaii, Barack Obama was the son of a Kenyan father and a white American mother. His parents divorced when he was young, and he was raised primarily by his mother and grandparents. Obama's multicultural upbringing would later shape his worldview and his approach to politics, as he sought to bridge divides and bring people together across lines of race, ethnicity, and ideology.

After graduating from Columbia University and Harvard Law School, Obama began his career as a community organizer in Chicago, where he worked with low-income communities to address issues such as job training, affordable housing, and access to healthcare. It was during this time that he developed a deep understanding of the challenges facing ordinary Americans and a passion for public service.

In 1996, Obama was elected to the Illinois State Senate, where he served with distinction for eight years, earning a reputation as a thoughtful and pragmatic lawmaker who was willing to reach across the aisle to get things done. In 2004, he burst onto the national stage with a stirring keynote address at the Democratic National Convention, where he spoke eloquently about the need to move beyond the politics of division and embrace a politics of unity and common purpose.

Buoyed by the success of his convention speech, Obama decided to run for the U.S. Senate, and in November 2004, he won a landslide victory, becoming only the third African American to be elected to the Senate since Reconstruction. In the Senate, Obama quickly established himself as a rising star within the Democratic Party, earning praise for his intelligence, charisma, and ability to work across party lines.

It was against this backdrop of political success and rising expectations that Obama announced his candidacy for president on February 10, 2007, in Springfield, Illinois, the same place where Abraham Lincoln had launched his own presidential campaign nearly 150 years earlier. In his announcement speech, Obama spoke movingly about his own journey and the challenges facing the nation, laying out a vision for a new kind of politics – one that was inclusive, hopeful, and focused on the common good.

From the outset, Obama's campaign struck a chord with millions of Americans who were hungry for change. His message of hope and optimism resonated deeply with voters of all backgrounds, as did his promise to bring a new kind of leadership to Washington – one that was honest, transparent, and accountable to the people.

As the primary season got underway, Obama faced off against a crowded field of Democratic contenders, including seasoned politicians like Hillary Clinton and John Edwards. Despite being relatively unknown on the national stage, Obama's grassroots campaign quickly gained momentum, fueled by a groundswell of support from young people, African Americans, and progressive activists.

Key to Obama's success was his ability to inspire and mobilize voters like never before. His rallies drew massive crowds wherever he went, and his speeches – delivered with passion, eloquence, and a touch of charisma – left audiences feeling energized and hopeful about the future. At the same time, his campaign made effective use of social media and grassroots organizing techniques to reach out to voters directly, bypassing traditional gatekeepers and engaging them in the political process in new and innovative ways.

By the time the Democratic primaries were over, Obama had emerged as the clear frontrunner, having won a decisive victory in both the popular vote and the delegate count. In June 2008, he clinched the Democratic nomination, becoming the first African American to lead a major party ticket for president.

As the general election campaign got underway, Obama faced off against Republican nominee John McCain, a veteran senator and war hero with a long record of service to his country. Despite McCain's formidable credentials and the lingering effects of racial prejudice in some parts of the country, Obama's message of hope and change continued to resonate with voters, and on November 4, 2008, he was elected the 44th President of the United States in a historic landslide victory.

As he stood before a jubilant crowd of supporters in Grant Park in Chicago on election night, Obama spoke of the challenges and opportunities that lay ahead, and he reiterated his commitment to bringing about the change that the American people had voted for. "This is your victory," he told the crowd. "It belongs to you."

And so began the Obama presidency – a momentous chapter in American history that would be defined by hope, change, and the audacity to believe that a better world was possible.

Chapter 2: The Campaign Trail

Obama's Historic Campaign: The Grassroots Movement, Message of Hope, and Mobilization of Young Voters

Barack Obama's campaign for the presidency in 2008 was not just a political campaign; it was a movement. From the very beginning, Obama and his team understood that they were not just running for office – they were running to change the world. And they did so by building one of the most innovative and effective grassroots campaigns in American history.

At the heart of Obama's campaign was a simple yet powerful message: hope and change. It was a message that resonated deeply with millions of Americans who were tired of the status quo, tired of politics as usual, and hungry for a leader who could offer them a vision of a better future. Obama's promise to bring a new kind of politics to Washington – one that was inclusive, transparent, and focused on the common good – struck a chord with voters of all backgrounds, and it became the rallying cry of his campaign.

But Obama's message of hope and change was more than just words; it was a call to action. From the very beginning, Obama made it clear that he couldn't bring about the change that the country needed on his own – he would need the help of ordinary Americans from all walks of life. And so, he set about building a grassroots movement unlike anything the country had ever seen.

At the heart of Obama's grassroots campaign were thousands of volunteers who dedicated their time, energy, and passion to spreading the word about Obama's candidacy and mobilizing voters in communities across the country. These volunteers, many of whom had never been involved in politics before, were the backbone of the Obama campaign, knocking on doors, making phone calls, and organizing events to get out the vote.

But Obama's grassroots movement wasn't just about winning elections; it was about building a lasting infrastructure for change. In addition to mobilizing voters, Obama's campaign also focused on empowering ordinary Americans to take ownership of the political process and become agents of change in their own communities. Through initiatives like "Obama Organizing Fellows" and "Camp Obama" training sessions, the campaign provided supporters with the tools, resources, and training they needed to become effective organizers and advocates for change.

One of the most remarkable aspects of Obama's grassroots campaign was its ability to mobilize young voters in unprecedented numbers. Inspired by Obama's message of hope and change, young people flocked to his campaign in droves, eager to be part of something bigger than themselves. Obama's team recognized the importance of young voters early on and made a concerted effort to engage them in the political process, using social media, grassroots organizing, and celebrity endorsements to reach out to this crucial demographic.

Key Moments and Speeches During the Campaign Trail

Throughout the campaign, Obama delivered a series of key moments and speeches that galvanized supporters, captured the imagination of the nation, and helped to define the narrative of his candidacy. From his historic announcement speech in Springfield, Illinois, to his stirring victory speech on election night, Obama's speeches were marked by their eloquence, passion, and ability to inspire hope in the face of adversity.

One of the defining moments of Obama's campaign came early on, in March 2008, when he delivered a speech on race in America in response to controversy surrounding his former pastor, Rev. Jeremiah Wright. In the speech, which became known as the "A More Perfect Union" speech, Obama spoke candidly about the legacy of slavery and segregation in America, the persistence of racial inequality, and the need for Americans of all races to come together to build a more just and inclusive society. The speech was hailed as a moment of honesty and courage, and it helped to defuse tensions surrounding the issue of race while reaffirming Obama's commitment to unity and reconciliation.

Another key moment in the campaign came in August 2008, when Obama accepted the Democratic nomination for president at the party's national convention in Denver, Colorado. In his acceptance speech, delivered before a crowd of thousands of enthusiastic supporters, Obama laid out his vision for America and his plans for addressing the challenges facing the nation. He spoke passionately about the need to rebuild the economy, expand access to healthcare, and restore America's standing in the world, and he called on Americans to come together as one nation to meet these challenges head-on.

But perhaps the most memorable moment of Obama's campaign came on election night, November 4, 2008, when he addressed a crowd of jubilant supporters in Grant Park in Chicago. In his victory speech, Obama spoke movingly about the historic significance of his election as the first African American president, and he thanked the American people for their faith and confidence in him. He also spoke of the challenges and opportunities that lay ahead, and he reiterated his commitment to bringing about the change that the country needed.

As Obama spoke, the crowd erupted in cheers and applause, waving American flags and chanting "Yes we can!" It was a moment of triumph and celebration, a moment that seemed to encapsulate the hope and optimism that had propelled Obama's campaign from the very beginning. And as the confetti fell and the music played, it was clear that a new era had dawned in American politics – an era of hope, change, and the audacity to believe that a better world was possible.

Chapter 3: Election Victory

The Excitement and Anticipation Leading up to Election Day

In the weeks and months leading up to Election Day on November 4, 2008, the United States was gripped by a sense of excitement and anticipation unlike anything the country had ever seen. From coast to coast, millions of Americans were energized and engaged in the political process, eager to cast their votes and be part of history. At the heart of this excitement was the historic candidacy of Barack Obama, whose campaign for the presidency had captured the imagination of the nation and inspired millions of people to believe in the possibility of change.

Throughout the campaign, Obama had run on a message of hope and change, promising to bring a new kind of politics to Washington and to unite the country around a common purpose. His message resonated deeply with voters, particularly young people, minorities, and progressives, who were hungry for a leader who could offer them a vision of a better future. As a result, Obama's campaign had generated an unprecedented level of enthusiasm and grassroots activism, with millions of volunteers working tirelessly to get out the vote and mobilize support for his candidacy.

In the days leading up to Election Day, the excitement reached a fever pitch, as Obama crisscrossed the country, holding rallies and campaign events in battleground states like Ohio, Florida, and Pennsylvania. At every stop, he was greeted by throngs of enthusiastic supporters, waving signs, chanting his name, and cheering him on with unbridled enthusiasm. It was a testament to the depth of support for Obama and the sense of urgency that many Americans felt about the need for change.

Meanwhile, Obama's opponent, Republican nominee John McCain, was waging a spirited campaign of his own, crisscrossing the country in a last-ditch effort to rally support for his candidacy. But despite McCain's best efforts, it was clear that the momentum was firmly on Obama's side, as evidenced by the large crowds and enthusiastic receptions that greeted him wherever he went. As Election Day drew nearer, the polls showed Obama with a commanding lead, both nationally and in key battleground states, leading many political pundits to predict a landslide victory for the Democratic candidate.

But while the excitement and anticipation were palpable, there was also a sense of apprehension and anxiety among Obama's supporters, who knew that the outcome of the election was far from certain. Memories of past disappointments – like the contested election of 2000 and the narrow defeat of John Kerry in 2004 – loomed large in the minds of many Democrats, who feared that victory could slip through their fingers at the last moment. As a result, Obama's campaign continued to work tirelessly to mobilize voters and get out the vote, leaving nothing to chance in the final days of the campaign.

Obama's Historic Win and the Significance of His Presidency as the First African American President

Finally, the long-awaited Election Day arrived, and Americans headed to the polls in record numbers to cast their votes for president. Lines stretched around the block at polling places across the country, as voters waited patiently for their chance to participate in the democratic process and make their voices heard. For many, it was a moment of pride and excitement, as they cast their ballots for the candidate of their choice and played a part in shaping the future of their country.

As the results began to pour in on election night, it quickly became clear that Obama was on the verge of making history. State after state turned blue as Obama racked up victories in key battlegrounds like Ohio, Florida, and Virginia, defying expectations and confounding his critics. And then, shortly before midnight, the networks called the election in Obama's favor, declaring him the winner of the 2008 presidential race.

The reaction was swift and jubilant, as supporters took to the streets to celebrate Obama's historic victory. In cities and towns across the country, crowds gathered in public squares and parks, waving American flags, singing songs, and dancing in the streets. It was a moment of triumph and joy, a moment that seemed to signal the dawn of a new era in American politics – an era of hope, change, and the audacity to believe that anything was possible.

For African Americans, Obama's victory was particularly poignant, as it marked the culmination of a long and difficult struggle for equality and justice. From the days of slavery and segregation to the civil rights movement of the 1960s, African Americans had fought for the right to participate fully in American democracy, and Obama's election as the first African American president was a symbol of how far the country had come – and how far it still had to go.

As Obama himself acknowledged in his victory speech, his election was about more than just him – it was about the millions of people who had worked and sacrificed to make it possible. It was about the parents and grandparents who had dreamed of a better future for their children, the activists and organizers who had fought for justice and equality, and the ordinary Americans who had believed in the possibility of change and had come together to make it happen.

But while Obama's victory was a cause for celebration, it was also a sobering reminder of the challenges that lay ahead. The country was facing the worst economic crisis since the Great Depression, with millions of Americans out of work and struggling to make ends meet. The wars in Iraq and Afghanistan were still raging, with no end in sight, and the country was deeply divided along partisan lines, with gridlock and dysfunction in Washington.

As Obama prepared to take office, he knew that he would be inheriting a nation in crisis – a nation that was hungry for change and desperate for leadership. But he also knew that he had the talent, the vision, and the determination to rise to the challenge and to lead the country forward into a brighter, more hopeful future. And as he stood before the American people on that historic night in November 2008, he pledged to do just that. "This is your victory," he told the crowd. "It belongs to you." And with those words, he set out to make good on his promise to bring hope and change to the 21st century.

Chapter 4: Inauguration and Early Days

The Inauguration Ceremony: Obama's Iconic Speech and the Symbolism of the Moment

On January 20, 2009, millions of Americans gathered on the National Mall in Washington, D.C., to witness history in the making as Barack Obama was sworn in as the 44th President of the United States. The atmosphere was electric, as a sea of people – young and old, black and white, Democrat and Republican – came together to celebrate the inauguration of the country's first African American president.

As Obama took the oath of office, administered by Chief Justice John Roberts, a hush fell over the crowd, broken only by the sound of applause and the occasional cheer. It was a moment of profound significance, not just for Obama and his family, but for the nation as a whole – a moment that symbolized how far the country had come and how much still remained to be done.

Following the oath of office, Obama delivered his inaugural address – a speech that would go down in history as one of the most memorable and inspiring ever delivered by an American president. In his address, Obama spoke eloquently about the challenges facing the nation and the need for unity and common purpose in the face of adversity.

"We gather here today," Obama began, "to affirm the greatness of our nation – not because of the height of our skyscrapers, or the power of our military, or the size of our economy – but because of the strength of our ideals: democracy, liberty, opportunity, and unyielding hope."

Throughout his speech, Obama struck a tone of optimism and determination, urging Americans to come together to tackle the pressing issues of the day – from the economic crisis and healthcare reform to climate change and national security. He spoke of the need to put aside partisan differences and work together in pursuit of a common purpose, invoking the spirit of unity and cooperation that had defined his campaign.

But perhaps the most memorable moment of Obama's speech came when he addressed the issue of race – a topic that had been central to his campaign and that continued to divide the country. "For we know that our patchwork heritage is a strength, not a weakness," Obama declared. "We are a nation of Christians and Muslims, Jews and Hindus – and non-believers. We are shaped by every language and culture, drawn from every end of this Earth."

It was a moment of profound symbolism, as Obama acknowledged the country's diversity and celebrated its multicultural heritage. And it was a reminder that, despite the challenges and divisions that lay ahead, America's greatest strength lay in its ability to come together as one nation, indivisible, with liberty and justice for all.

As Obama concluded his speech, the crowd erupted in cheers and applause, waving American flags and chanting his name. It was a moment of hope and inspiration, a moment that seemed to signal the dawn of a new era in American politics – an era of hope, change, and the audacity to believe that anything was possible.

Early Challenges and Decisions Faced by the New Administration

But as the euphoria of the inauguration gave way to the realities of governing, Obama and his team faced a daunting array of challenges and decisions in the early days of his administration. Chief among these was the economy, which was teetering on the brink of collapse in the wake of the 2008 financial crisis.

In response to the crisis, Obama wasted no time in taking action, pushing Congress to pass a massive economic stimulus package aimed at jumpstarting the economy and creating jobs. The $787 billion package, known as the American Recovery and Reinvestment Act, included funding for infrastructure projects, tax cuts for middle-class families, and aid to states and local governments.

But while the stimulus package helped to stabilize the economy and prevent a full-blown depression, it was not without its critics, who argued that it was too expensive and that it did not go far enough to address the root causes of the crisis. Obama's decision to bail out the auto industry was also controversial, with many Republicans and conservatives accusing him of overreach and government intervention in the free market.

In addition to the economy, Obama also faced a number of other pressing issues in the early days of his administration, including healthcare reform, climate change, and national security. On healthcare, Obama made it clear that he was committed to fulfilling his campaign promise of expanding access to affordable healthcare for all Americans, and he worked closely with Congress to draft and pass the Affordable Care Act (ACA), also known as Obamacare.

The ACA, which was signed into law in March 2010, represented the most significant overhaul of the American healthcare system in decades, expanding coverage to millions of uninsured Americans, prohibiting insurance companies from denying coverage based on pre-existing conditions, and instituting a number of other reforms aimed at reducing costs and improving quality of care. But like the stimulus package, the ACA was deeply divisive, with Republicans and conservatives launching a concerted effort to repeal it, culminating in a series of legal challenges that ultimately made their way to the Supreme Court.

On climate change, Obama faced resistance from Republicans and industry groups opposed to government regulation of greenhouse gas emissions. Nevertheless, he pressed ahead with efforts to address the issue, implementing a series of executive actions aimed at reducing carbon pollution, promoting clean energy, and protecting the environment. He also played a key role in negotiating the Paris

Agreement, a landmark international accord aimed at limiting global warming and mitigating its effects.

Finally, on national security, Obama faced the ongoing challenges of the wars in Iraq and Afghanistan, as well as the threat of terrorism at home and abroad. In his first days in office, he signed an executive order to close the Guantanamo Bay detention facility, fulfilling a campaign promise to end the use of torture and uphold the rule of law. He also ordered a review of U.S. counterterrorism policies and practices, with a focus on protecting civil liberties and promoting transparency and accountability.

But despite his early successes and accomplishments, Obama faced an uphill battle in Congress, where partisan gridlock and obstructionism threatened to derail his agenda at every turn. Nevertheless, he remained undeterred, pressing forward with his efforts to bring about the change that the country needed, and laying the groundwork for a legacy that would endure long after his time in office had come to an end.

Chapter 5: Economic Crisis and Recovery

Obama's Response to the 2008 Financial Crisis: The Stimulus Package and Efforts to Stabilize the Economy

When Barack Obama took office as President of the United States in January 2009, he inherited an economy in freefall. The 2008 financial crisis, triggered by the collapse of the housing market and the subsequent implosion of major financial institutions like Lehman Brothers, had plunged the country into the deepest recession since the Great Depression. Millions of Americans had lost their jobs, homes, and life savings, and the country was teetering on the brink of economic collapse.

In response to the crisis, Obama and his economic team wasted no time in taking action. Their goal was clear: to stabilize the economy, restore confidence in the financial system, and put America back to work. To achieve this, they proposed a bold and ambitious plan – the American Recovery and Reinvestment Act (ARRA) – a massive stimulus package aimed at jumpstarting economic growth and creating jobs.

The ARRA, which was signed into law by Obama in February 2009, represented the largest investment in infrastructure, education, healthcare, and renewable energy in American history. It included funding for projects like road and bridge repair, school construction, and clean energy development, as well as tax cuts for middle-class families and aid to states and local governments struggling with budget deficits.

The impact of the stimulus package was immediate and far-reaching. Millions of jobs were created or saved, as construction crews went to work repairing roads and bridges, teachers were hired to reduce class sizes, and firefighters and police officers were kept on the job. The unemployment rate, which had peaked at 10% in October 2009, began to decline steadily, and the economy began to grow again, albeit slowly.

But perhaps the most important aspect of the stimulus package was its role in preventing a full-blown depression. By injecting hundreds of billions of dollars into the economy, the ARRA helped to stabilize financial markets, restore confidence in the banking system, and prevent a downward spiral of deflation and economic collapse. It was a bold and controversial move, but one that many economists credit with preventing a second Great Depression and laying the groundwork for the economic recovery that followed.

Criticisms and Controversies Surrounding the Administration's Economic Policies

Despite its successes, the ARRA was not without its critics. From the outset, Republicans and conservatives denounced the stimulus package as wasteful government spending that would do little to stimulate economic growth and create jobs. They argued that the package was too expensive, too focused on government intervention in the economy, and too laden with pork-barrel projects and special-interest giveaways.

These criticisms were fueled by a number of high-profile controversies surrounding the administration's economic policies, including the failure of several high-profile companies that received bailout funds, such as AIG and General Motors. Critics pointed to these failures as evidence of the government's inability to effectively manage the economy and questioned the wisdom of using taxpayer dollars to prop up failing businesses.

But perhaps the biggest controversy surrounding the administration's economic policies was the debate over the effectiveness of the stimulus package itself. While supporters of the package point to the millions of jobs created or saved and the steady decline in the unemployment rate as evidence of its success, critics argue that the recovery was too slow and too uneven, and that much of the money was wasted on pet projects and ineffective programs.

One of the most common criticisms of the stimulus package was that it was too small to adequately address the scale of the crisis. Many economists argued that the package should have been larger and more targeted, with a greater emphasis on direct assistance to struggling homeowners and small businesses. They also criticized the administration for failing to address the underlying causes of the crisis, such as the deregulation of the financial industry and the proliferation of risky lending practices.

Another source of controversy was the administration's handling of the housing market, which continued to languish in the wake of the crisis. Despite efforts to help struggling homeowners through programs like the Home Affordable Modification Program (HAMP), millions of Americans lost their homes to foreclosure, and the housing market remained mired in a slump for years.

In addition to these criticisms, the administration also faced backlash over its handling of the auto industry bailout, which was seen by many as a government takeover of private industry. While the bailout ultimately saved thousands of jobs and helped to prevent the collapse of the American auto industry, it was deeply unpopular with many Americans, who saw it as an example of government overreach and corporate welfare.

But despite these controversies, the Obama administration's economic policies ultimately succeeded in stabilizing the economy, preventing a second Great Depression, and laying the groundwork for the economic recovery that followed. While the recovery was slow and uneven, particularly for those hardest hit by the recession, it nevertheless represented a remarkable turnaround from the depths of the crisis, and a testament to the resilience and strength of the American economy.

Chapter 6: Healthcare Reform

The Fight for Healthcare Reform: Obama's Push for the Affordable Care Act (ACA)

From the moment he took office, healthcare reform was one of Barack Obama's top priorities. For decades, the United States had grappled with the challenge of providing affordable, accessible healthcare to all its citizens, and Obama was determined to tackle this issue head-on. Building on decades of advocacy and debate, Obama and his administration embarked on a historic push to enact comprehensive healthcare reform that would expand coverage, control costs, and improve the quality of care for millions of Americans.

The fight for healthcare reform began in earnest in early 2009, as Obama and his team worked with Congress to draft and pass legislation aimed at achieving these ambitious goals. Drawing on input from healthcare experts, economists, and stakeholders from across the political spectrum, they crafted a comprehensive plan that would come to be known as the Affordable Care Act (ACA), or Obamacare.

At the heart of the ACA was a series of key provisions aimed at expanding access to healthcare for millions of Americans who were uninsured or underinsured. These provisions included:

1. The creation of health insurance exchanges where individuals and small businesses could shop for and compare insurance plans, with subsidies available to help lower-income individuals and families afford coverage.

2. The expansion of Medicaid to cover millions of low-income adults who had previously been excluded from the program.

3. Prohibitions on insurance companies from denying coverage or charging higher premiums based on pre-existing conditions, as well as caps on out-of-pocket expenses.

4. Requirements for individuals to have health insurance coverage or face a penalty, known as the individual mandate.

In addition to these coverage expansions, the ACA also included a number of provisions aimed at controlling costs and improving the quality of care. These provisions included incentives for healthcare providers to adopt electronic medical records, initiatives to promote preventive care and wellness programs, and efforts to reduce waste, fraud, and abuse in the healthcare system.

But while the goals of the ACA were laudable, the road to passage would prove to be long and contentious. From the outset, Republicans and conservatives mounted a fierce opposition to the legislation, accusing Obama of pushing a government takeover of healthcare and warning of dire consequences for the economy and the quality of care.

The battle reached a fever pitch in the summer of 2009, as lawmakers returned to their home districts for the August recess and were met with a wave of protests and town hall meetings organized by opponents of the ACA. Angry constituents confronted their representatives, accusing them of supporting a socialist takeover of healthcare and demanding that they vote against the legislation.

But despite the heated rhetoric and intense opposition, Obama and his allies in Congress pressed forward with their efforts to pass the ACA. In November 2009, the House of Representatives narrowly passed its version of the bill, followed by the Senate in December. But the real challenge lay ahead in reconciling the two versions and securing enough votes to pass a final bill.

The turning point came in March 2010, when Obama convened a historic summit at the White House with Democratic and Republican leaders to discuss healthcare reform. Despite their ideological differences, the two sides engaged in a frank and open dialogue about the challenges facing the healthcare system and the need for bipartisan solutions. While the summit did not produce any breakthroughs, it helped to create a sense of momentum and urgency around the issue, and in the weeks that followed, Democrats in Congress rallied behind a final push to pass the ACA.

On March 21, 2010, after months of negotiations and wrangling, the House of Representatives passed the final version of the ACA by a narrow margin, with not a single Republican voting in favor. The bill was then sent to the Senate, where it passed by a similarly narrow margin, with Vice President Joe Biden casting the tie-breaking vote.

The passage of the ACA was a historic moment in American history, marking the culmination of decades of struggle and debate over healthcare reform. For Obama and his supporters, it was a moment of triumph and vindication, as they succeeded where so many others had failed in achieving comprehensive healthcare reform.

Passage of the ACA and its Impact on American Healthcare

The passage of the ACA had a profound and far-reaching impact on American healthcare, touching the lives of millions of individuals and families across the country. In the years since its enactment, the ACA has transformed the healthcare landscape in numerous ways, expanding coverage, controlling costs, and improving the quality of care for millions of Americans.

One of the most significant achievements of the ACA was its success in expanding access to healthcare coverage. Since its passage, millions of previously uninsured individuals and families have gained access to affordable, comprehensive health insurance coverage through the health insurance exchanges and the expansion of Medicaid. According to the U.S. Census Bureau, the uninsured rate in the United States fell from 16% in 2010 to 8.7% in 2016, representing a historic low.

The ACA also brought about important changes in the way healthcare is delivered and paid for in the United States. The law introduced a number of reforms aimed at controlling costs and improving the quality of care, such as incentives for healthcare providers to adopt electronic medical records, initiatives to promote preventive care and wellness programs, and efforts to reduce waste, fraud, and abuse in the healthcare system. These reforms have helped to slow the growth of healthcare spending and improve patient outcomes, while also increasing transparency and accountability in the healthcare system.

In addition to expanding coverage and controlling costs, the ACA also introduced a number of important consumer protections aimed at ensuring that all Americans have access to high-quality, affordable healthcare. These protections include prohibitions on insurance companies from denying coverage or charging higher premiums based on pre-existing conditions, as well as caps on out-of-pocket expenses. The ACA also extended coverage for young adults by allowing them to stay on their parents' insurance plans until age 26, providing critical financial support for millions of young people as they transition into adulthood.

But while the ACA has been successful in expanding coverage and improving access to healthcare for millions of Americans, it has also faced its fair share of challenges and controversies. From the outset, the law has been the subject of fierce political debate, with Republicans and conservatives launching repeated efforts to repeal or undermine it. These efforts have included legal challenges, congressional investigations, and attempts to defund key provisions of the law, such as the individual mandate and the Medicaid expansion.

In addition to political opposition, the ACA has also faced challenges in implementation, with some states opting not to expand Medicaid or establish their own health insurance exchanges, leaving millions of Americans without access to affordable coverage. There have also been concerns about rising premiums and deductibles, particularly for individuals and families who do not qualify for subsidies through the exchanges.

Nevertheless, despite these challenges, the ACA remains a landmark achievement in American healthcare policy, representing a significant step forward in the ongoing struggle to ensure that all Americans have access to high-quality, affordable healthcare. As Obama himself declared on the day the ACA was signed into law, "This is a victory for every American who has been told they can't afford health insurance, or that their pre-existing condition makes them uninsurable. This is a victory for the American people." And indeed, the ACA has changed the lives of millions of Americans for the better, ensuring that they have access to the care they need, when they need it, regardless of their income, health status, or background.

Chapter 7: Foreign Policy Challenges

Obama's Approach to Foreign Policy: Diplomacy, Engagement, and Multilateralism

When Barack Obama took office as President of the United States in January 2009, he inherited a world in turmoil. From the ongoing wars in Iraq and Afghanistan to the growing threat of terrorism and the specter of nuclear proliferation, the challenges facing American foreign policy were daunting and complex. But Obama was determined to chart a new course – one characterized by diplomacy, engagement, and multilateralism – in pursuit of a safer, more stable world.

From the outset, Obama made it clear that he believed in the power of diplomacy to resolve conflicts and advance American interests. He rejected the unilateralist approach of his predecessor, George W. Bush, in favor of a more nuanced and pragmatic approach that sought to engage with allies and adversaries alike to address shared challenges and promote peace and prosperity.

One of the central pillars of Obama's foreign policy was his commitment to multilateralism – the idea that complex global problems require collective solutions and that the United States cannot go it alone in tackling the world's most pressing challenges. Throughout his presidency, Obama worked tirelessly to strengthen international institutions like the United Nations, NATO, and the World Trade Organization, and to forge partnerships and alliances with other countries to address issues ranging from climate change and nuclear proliferation to terrorism and global health.

But perhaps the most distinctive aspect of Obama's approach to foreign policy was his emphasis on engagement – the idea that the United States should seek to build bridges, not walls, with other nations, and that dialogue and diplomacy are the best tools for resolving conflicts and promoting peace. From his historic outreach to the Muslim world in his Cairo speech in 2009 to his efforts to normalize relations with Cuba in 2014, Obama consistently sought to engage with America's adversaries and adversaries in pursuit of common goals.

Major Events and Crises During Obama's Presidency, Including the Arab Spring, Iran Nuclear Deal, and Osama bin Laden's Death

During his eight years in office, Barack Obama faced a series of major events and crises on the world stage that tested his leadership and shaped his foreign policy legacy. From the Arab Spring and the civil war in Syria to the Iran nuclear deal and the killing of Osama bin Laden, these events would leave an indelible mark on the course of history and the future of American foreign policy.

The Arab Spring

One of the defining moments of Obama's presidency came in 2011, with the outbreak of the Arab Spring – a wave of popular uprisings and protests that swept across the Middle East and North Africa, toppling authoritarian regimes and demanding greater political freedom and economic opportunity. From Tunisia and Egypt to Libya and Syria, millions of people took to the streets to demand an end to corruption, repression, and tyranny, and to call for democratic reform.

In response to the Arab Spring, Obama faced a delicate balancing act – on the one hand, he sought to support the aspirations of the protesters and promote democracy and human rights in the region, while on the other hand, he had to navigate the complex geopolitical realities of the Middle East and avoid destabilizing the region further. Throughout the Arab Spring, Obama and his administration worked closely with allies and partners to support peaceful transitions to democracy and to push for political and economic reforms in countries undergoing political upheaval.

One of the most challenging cases was Syria, where the government of President Bashar al-Assad brutally suppressed protests and unleashed a wave of violence against civilians. Despite widespread calls for international intervention to stop the bloodshed, Obama resisted pressure to intervene militarily, fearing that military action could escalate the conflict and draw the United States into another costly and protracted war in the Middle East. Instead, he pursued a policy of diplomatic engagement and support for the Syrian opposition, while also working with allies to provide humanitarian assistance to the millions of Syrians displaced by the conflict.

The Iran Nuclear Deal

Another major foreign policy challenge facing Obama was the question of Iran's nuclear program and the threat of nuclear proliferation in the Middle East. For years, the international community had been locked in a standoff with Iran over its nuclear ambitions, with the United States and its allies demanding that Iran abandon its nuclear program and Iran insisting on its right to develop nuclear technology for peaceful purposes.

In 2015, after years of negotiations and diplomacy, Obama and his administration achieved a historic breakthrough with the signing of the Joint Comprehensive Plan of Action (JCPOA), also known as the Iran nuclear deal. Under the terms of the agreement, Iran agreed to limit its nuclear activities and submit to strict international inspections in exchange for the lifting of economic sanctions and the normalization of relations with the United States and other countries.

The Iran nuclear deal was hailed as a major diplomatic achievement, one that had the potential to avert a nuclear arms race in the Middle East and pave the way for greater stability and cooperation in the region. But it was also deeply controversial, with critics arguing that it did not go far enough in curbing Iran's nuclear ambitions and that it emboldened Iran to pursue its aggressive behavior in the region.

Despite these criticisms, Obama and his administration remained committed to the Iran nuclear deal, arguing that it represented the best chance for preventing Iran from obtaining nuclear weapons and reducing the risk of a catastrophic conflict in the region. And while the future of the deal remains uncertain in the wake of the Trump administration's decision to withdraw from it in 2018, its legacy as a landmark achievement in diplomacy and nonproliferation will endure.

Osama bin Laden's Death

On May 1, 2011, the world received news that Osama bin Laden, the mastermind behind the September 11, 2001, terrorist attacks that killed nearly 3,000 people, had been killed in a covert operation by U.S. Navy SEALS in Pakistan. The news of bin Laden's death sent shockwaves around the world and was met with widespread jubilation and relief, as people across the globe celebrated the demise of one of the most notorious terrorists in history.

For Obama, bin Laden's death was a defining moment in his presidency – a moment that demonstrated America's resolve and determination to bring terrorists to justice, no matter how long it took. In a late-night address to the nation, Obama hailed bin Laden's death as a "major victory" in the fight against terrorism and a testament to the bravery and skill of America's military and intelligence professionals.

But while bin Laden's death was a significant milestone in the fight against terrorism, it did not mark the end of the threat. In the years that followed, the United States continued to face a range of security challenges, from the rise of ISIS in Iraq and Syria to the spread of violent extremism and radicalization online. And while Obama and his administration made significant progress in degrading and defeating terrorist organizations like al-Qaeda and ISIS, the fight against terrorism remained a top priority for American foreign policy.

In conclusion, Barack Obama's approach to foreign policy was characterized by diplomacy, engagement, and multilateralism – a departure from the unilateralism and militarism of his predecessor. From the Arab Spring and the Iran nuclear deal to the killing of Osama bin Laden, Obama faced a series of major events and crises on the world stage that tested his leadership and shaped his foreign policy legacy. And while his presidency was not without its challenges and controversies, his commitment to dialogue and cooperation laid the groundwork for a more peaceful and prosperous world for future generations.

Chapter 8: Climate Change and Environmental Policy

Obama's Efforts to Address Climate Change and Promote Environmental Sustainability

As Barack Obama took office as President of the United States in January 2009, he faced an urgent and pressing challenge – the threat of climate change and the need to transition to a more sustainable and environmentally friendly economy. From rising temperatures and extreme weather events to melting ice caps and disappearing forests, the impacts of climate change were becoming increasingly evident and alarming, and the need for action was clear.

From the outset, Obama made addressing climate change a top priority of his administration. He recognized that the United States had a moral obligation to lead the fight against climate change, both for the sake of future generations and for the sake of the planet itself. And he was determined to take bold and decisive action to reduce greenhouse gas emissions, promote renewable energy, and protect the environment for years to come.

One of the central pillars of Obama's efforts to address climate change was his commitment to reducing greenhouse gas emissions from the burning of fossil fuels – the primary driver of climate change. To achieve this goal, Obama implemented a series of policies and initiatives aimed at transitioning to a cleaner, more sustainable energy future.

One of the most significant of these initiatives was the Clean Power Plan, which aimed to reduce carbon dioxide emissions from power plants – the largest source of greenhouse gas emissions in the United States. Under the Clean Power Plan, the Environmental Protection Agency (EPA) set strict limits on carbon emissions from existing power plants and provided incentives for states to transition to cleaner sources of energy, such as wind, solar, and nuclear power.

In addition to the Clean Power Plan, Obama also took a number of other actions to promote renewable energy and reduce dependence on fossil fuels. He expanded tax credits and incentives for renewable energy projects, invested in research and development of clean energy technologies, and worked to modernize the nation's energy infrastructure to make it more resilient to the impacts of climate change.

But perhaps the most significant action Obama took to address climate change was his decision to join the international community in negotiating the Paris Agreement – a landmark accord aimed at limiting global warming to well below 2 degrees Celsius above pre-industrial levels and pursuing efforts to limit the temperature increase to 1.5 degrees Celsius. In December 2015, representatives from nearly 200 countries came together in Paris to negotiate the agreement, which was hailed as a historic breakthrough in the fight against climate change.

Implementation of Policies such as the Clean Power Plan and the Paris Agreement

The implementation of policies such as the Clean Power Plan and the Paris Agreement represented a significant step forward in the fight against climate change, but it was not without its challenges and controversies.

The Clean Power Plan, in particular, faced fierce opposition from the fossil fuel industry and conservative lawmakers, who argued that it would kill jobs, raise energy prices, and undermine the economy. In 2016, the Supreme Court issued a stay on the implementation of the Clean Power Plan pending legal challenges, effectively halting its progress and leaving its future uncertain.

Similarly, the Paris Agreement faced criticism from skeptics who questioned its effectiveness and criticized the United States for committing to emissions reductions while allowing countries like China and India to continue increasing their emissions. In June 2017, President Donald Trump announced that the United States would withdraw from the agreement, fulfilling a campaign promise to prioritize the interests of the fossil fuel industry over the global fight against climate change.

Despite these setbacks, however, the momentum for action on climate change continued to grow, both domestically and internationally. In the United States, cities, states, and businesses stepped up to fill the leadership void left by the federal government, committing to ambitious emissions reduction targets and investing in renewable energy and energy efficiency projects. Internationally, other countries reaffirmed their commitment to the Paris Agreement, vowing to continue working together to address the urgent threat of climate change.

And while the road ahead remains challenging, there is reason for optimism. The cost of renewable energy continues to plummet, making it increasingly competitive with fossil fuels. Public awareness of the dangers of climate change is growing, with polls showing that a majority of Americans now believe that action is needed to address the issue. And a new generation of activists and leaders is emerging, demanding bold and decisive action to tackle the greatest challenge of our time.

In conclusion, Barack Obama's efforts to address climate change and promote environmental sustainability represented a significant step forward in the fight against one of the greatest challenges of our time. From the implementation of policies like the Clean Power Plan to the negotiation of the Paris Agreement, Obama demonstrated bold and decisive leadership in confronting the urgent threat of climate change and laying the groundwork for a more sustainable and prosperous future for generations to come. And while the fight is far from over, Obama's legacy as a champion of climate action and environmental stewardship will endure as a beacon of hope and inspiration for future generations.

Chapter 9: Social Justice and Civil Rights

Obama's Advocacy for Social Justice and Civil Rights: Initiatives on Racial Equality, LGBTQ Rights, and Criminal Justice Reform

Barack Obama's presidency was marked by a deep commitment to social justice and civil rights, and his administration worked tirelessly to advance the cause of equality and justice for all Americans. From his advocacy for racial equality and LGBTQ rights to his efforts to reform the criminal justice system, Obama's presidency saw significant progress on a range of social justice issues. But it also faced challenges and setbacks along the way, as entrenched inequalities and systemic injustices continued to plague the nation.

Racial Equality

From the moment he took office, Barack Obama understood the significance of his historic presidency as the first African American to hold the highest office in the land. He recognized that his election was not the end of the struggle for racial equality, but rather the beginning of a new chapter in the fight for civil rights. And he was determined to use his position of power and influence to advance the cause of racial justice and equality for all Americans.

One of the central pillars of Obama's advocacy for racial equality was his commitment to closing the opportunity gap – the disparities in education, employment, housing, and healthcare that disproportionately affect communities of color. Throughout his presidency, Obama worked to address these disparities through a range of initiatives and programs aimed at expanding access to opportunity and breaking down barriers to success.

One of the most significant of these initiatives was the My Brother's Keeper initiative, launched by Obama in 2014 to address the opportunity gap facing young men of color. The initiative brought together government, businesses, nonprofits, and community organizations to develop and implement strategies to improve outcomes for young men of color in areas like education, employment, and criminal justice. Through partnerships and investments in programs like early childhood education, mentorship, and job training, My Brother's Keeper aimed to provide young men of color with the support and resources they need to succeed in life.

In addition to the My Brother's Keeper initiative, Obama also took a number of other actions to address racial disparities in areas like education, housing, and healthcare. He worked to expand access to quality education for all students, regardless of race or income, through initiatives like Race to the Top and Investing in Innovation. He fought to strengthen and enforce fair housing laws to ensure that all Americans have access to safe, affordable housing in neighborhoods of their choice. And he worked to expand access to healthcare for millions of Americans through the Affordable Care Act, which has disproportionately benefited communities of color who were previously uninsured or underinsured.

But perhaps the most significant aspect of Obama's advocacy for racial equality was his willingness to confront the issue of systemic racism head-on – to acknowledge that racism is not just a relic of the past, but a present-day reality that continues to shape the lives and experiences of millions of Americans. From his speech on race in Philadelphia in 2008 to his remarks on the shooting of Trayvon Martin in 2012, Obama used his platform as president to initiate difficult conversations about race and racism in America and to challenge the nation to live up to its ideals of equality and justice for all.

LGBTQ Rights

In addition to his advocacy for racial equality, Barack Obama was also a staunch advocate for LGBTQ rights, and his presidency saw significant progress on a range of issues affecting the LGBTQ community. From his support for marriage equality to his efforts to combat discrimination and violence against LGBTQ individuals, Obama worked to advance the cause of LGBTQ rights and ensure that all Americans are treated with dignity, respect, and equality under the law.

One of the most significant achievements of Obama's presidency was his decision to publicly support marriage equality – a historic moment that marked a major turning point in the fight for LGBTQ rights. In May 2012, Obama became the first sitting president to announce his support for marriage equality, stating in an interview with ABC News that "same-sex couples should be able to get married." His endorsement of marriage equality helped to shift public opinion on the issue and paved the way for the Supreme Court's landmark decision in Obergefell v. Hodges in 2015, which legalized same-sex marriage nationwide.

But Obama's advocacy for LGBTQ rights went beyond marriage equality. Throughout his presidency, he took a number of other actions to advance LGBTQ rights and combat discrimination and violence against LGBTQ individuals. He signed into law the Matthew Shepard and James Byrd Jr. Hate Crimes Prevention Act, which expanded federal hate crimes law to include crimes motivated by sexual orientation and gender identity. He repealed the military's discriminatory "Don't Ask, Don't Tell" policy, allowing gay and lesbian service members to serve openly in the military. And he took steps to protect LGBTQ individuals from discrimination in areas like housing, employment, and healthcare, issuing executive orders and supporting legislation to prohibit discrimination on the basis of sexual orientation and gender identity.

But despite these advances, the fight for LGBTQ rights is far from over, and Obama's presidency faced its share of challenges and setbacks along the way. The Supreme Court's decision in Obergefell v. Hodges was a major victory for marriage equality, but it did not address the full range of issues facing the LGBTQ community, including discrimination in areas like housing, employment, and healthcare. And while Obama took steps to address these issues through executive actions and administrative measures, progress on LGBTQ rights remained slow and uneven, with many states continuing to resist efforts to expand legal protections for LGBTQ individuals.

Criminal Justice Reform

In addition to his advocacy for racial equality and LGBTQ rights, Barack Obama was also a vocal advocate for criminal justice reform, recognizing the need to address the systemic injustices and inequalities that pervade the nation's criminal justice system. From mass incarceration and police brutality to racial profiling and disparities in sentencing, Obama sought to reform the criminal justice system from top to bottom and ensure that it is fair, just, and equitable for all Americans.

One of the central pillars of Obama's criminal justice reform agenda was his commitment to reducing mass incarceration – the phenomenon of locking up millions of Americans, disproportionately people of color, for nonviolent offenses. Throughout his presidency, Obama worked to address this issue through a range of initiatives and reforms aimed at reducing the number of people in prison, reforming sentencing laws, and investing in alternatives to incarceration.

One of the most significant of these initiatives was the Fair Sentencing Act, signed into law by Obama in 2010, which aimed to reduce the disparity in sentences for crack cocaine and powder cocaine offenses – a disparity that disproportionately affected African American defendants. The law reduced the sentencing disparity from 100:1 to 18:1, bringing greater fairness and equity to the criminal justice system.

In addition to the Fair Sentencing Act, Obama also took a number of other actions to reform the criminal justice system and address disparities in sentencing and law enforcement. He launched the Smart on Crime initiative, which aimed to prioritize the prosecution of violent and serious offenders while diverting nonviolent offenders into alternative programs like drug courts and rehabilitation programs. He issued executive orders to ban the use of solitary confinement for juveniles in federal prisons and to prohibit federal agencies from asking job applicants about their criminal histories until later in the hiring process.

But perhaps the most significant aspect of Obama's criminal justice reform agenda was his efforts to address police brutality and racial profiling – issues that have long plagued communities of color and strained relations between law enforcement and the communities they serve. Throughout his presidency, Obama spoke out against police brutality and racial profiling, calling for greater accountability and transparency in law enforcement and advocating for reforms to promote trust and cooperation between police and the communities they serve.

Despite these efforts, however, progress on criminal justice reform remained slow and uneven, and Obama's presidency faced its share of challenges and setbacks along the way. The Black Lives Matter movement, which emerged in response to police shootings of unarmed African Americans, brought renewed attention to issues of racial injustice and police violence, sparking protests and demonstrations across the country and demanding action to address systemic racism and inequality in the criminal justice system.

In conclusion, Barack Obama's presidency was marked by a deep commitment to social justice and civil rights, and his administration worked tirelessly to advance the cause of equality and justice for all Americans. From his advocacy for racial equality and LGBTQ rights to his efforts to reform the criminal justice system, Obama's presidency saw significant progress on a range of social justice issues. But it also faced challenges and setbacks along the way, as entrenched inequalities and systemic injustices continued to plague the nation. And while much work remains to be done to achieve the vision of a more just, equitable, and inclusive society, Obama's legacy as a champion of social justice and civil rights will endure as a beacon of hope and inspiration for future generations.

Chapter 10: Immigration Reform

Barack Obama's attempts to reform immigration policy, including the Deferred Action for Childhood Arrivals (DACA) program, marked a significant chapter in his presidency. Throughout his time in office, Obama faced intense pressure to address the nation's broken immigration system, which had long been a source of controversy and debate. With millions of undocumented immigrants living and working in the United States, and with families being torn apart by deportation, the need for comprehensive immigration reform was urgent and undeniable. Obama recognized this reality and made it a priority of his administration to push for meaningful reform that would provide a path to citizenship for undocumented immigrants, secure the border, and uphold America's values as a nation of immigrants.

However, Obama's efforts to reform immigration policy were met with fierce opposition from Republicans in Congress, who accused him of overstepping his authority and failing to enforce immigration laws. Despite repeated attempts to negotiate with lawmakers and find bipartisan solutions, Obama's immigration reform agenda was repeatedly stymied by partisan gridlock and political polarization. Nevertheless, he persisted in his efforts to address the issue, using executive action and administrative measures to make progress where legislative action proved impossible.

One of the most significant initiatives undertaken by the Obama administration to address immigration reform was the Deferred Action for Childhood Arrivals (DACA) program, which was announced in June 2012. DACA was designed to provide temporary relief from deportation and work authorization to undocumented immigrants who were brought to the United States as children – often referred to as Dreamers – and who met certain eligibility criteria, such as being enrolled in school or serving in the military. The program was a lifeline for hundreds of thousands of young immigrants who had grown up in the United States and considered it their home, offering them a chance to come out of the shadows and pursue their dreams without fear of deportation.

DACA was met with widespread praise and support from immigrant rights advocates, who hailed it as a compassionate and common-sense solution to the plight of Dreamers. But it also sparked fierce opposition from conservatives and anti-immigrant activists, who accused Obama of granting "amnesty" to undocumented immigrants and undermining the rule of law. The controversy surrounding DACA only intensified in September 2017, when President Donald Trump announced his decision to rescind the program, throwing the lives of hundreds of thousands of Dreamers into turmoil and reigniting the debate over immigration reform.

Despite the setbacks and challenges, Obama's efforts to reform immigration policy had a lasting impact on the national conversation surrounding immigration and laid the groundwork for future reform efforts. His advocacy for DACA and other initiatives to protect undocumented immigrants from deportation helped to shine a spotlight on the plight of millions of immigrants living in the shadows and galvanized support for comprehensive immigration reform. And while the fight for immigration reform is far from over, Obama's legacy as a champion of immigrant rights and a voice for compassion and inclusion will endure as a beacon of hope for immigrants and their families across the country.

Controversies and debates surrounding immigration during Obama's presidency were fueled by a combination of factors, including the polarized political climate, economic anxieties, and fears about national security. Throughout his presidency, Obama faced intense scrutiny and criticism from both sides of the political aisle over his handling of immigration issues, with conservatives accusing him of being too lenient on enforcement and liberals accusing him of not doing enough to protect immigrant rights.

One of the most contentious issues surrounding immigration during Obama's presidency was the surge of unaccompanied minors crossing the southern border in 2014. The influx of children fleeing violence and poverty in Central America overwhelmed immigration authorities and sparked a humanitarian crisis, with thousands of children being detained in overcrowded and unsanitary detention facilities along the border. The crisis drew sharp criticism from both Republicans and Democrats, who accused the Obama administration of failing to adequately address the root causes of the surge and of mishandling the response.

Another controversial issue surrounding immigration during Obama's presidency was the use of deportations as a tool of immigration enforcement. While Obama was often criticized by immigrant rights advocates for his record on deportations – which reached record highs during his first term in office – he also faced criticism from conservatives for not being tough enough on enforcement. The debate over deportations highlighted the difficult balancing act that Obama faced in trying to enforce immigration laws while also upholding America's values as a nation of immigrants.

But perhaps the most controversial immigration issue during Obama's presidency was the question of undocumented immigrants living and working in the United States. Despite repeated attempts to pass comprehensive immigration reform legislation that would provide a path to citizenship for undocumented immigrants, Obama was unable to overcome opposition from Republicans in Congress, who accused him of amnesty and refused to negotiate in good faith. As a result, Obama was forced to take unilateral action to address the issue, using executive orders and administrative measures to provide relief to certain groups of undocumented immigrants, such as Dreamers and parents of U.S. citizens and lawful permanent residents.

Obama's actions on immigration were met with fierce opposition from conservatives and anti-immigrant activists, who accused him of overstepping his authority and circumventing the will of Congress. The controversy surrounding Obama's immigration policies only intensified in the years that followed, culminating in a series of legal challenges and executive actions by the Trump administration to roll back Obama-era immigration policies and enact harsher enforcement measures.

In conclusion, Barack Obama's attempts to reform immigration policy during his presidency were marked by controversy, debate, and political polarization. Despite facing fierce opposition from Republicans in Congress and anti-immigrant activists, Obama remained steadfast in his commitment to advancing the cause of immigrant rights and pushing for comprehensive immigration reform. And while his efforts ultimately fell short of achieving the sweeping changes that he had hoped for, Obama's legacy as a champion of immigrant rights and a voice for compassion and inclusion will endure as a reminder of the importance of standing up for the most vulnerable members of society.

Chapter 11: Midterm Elections and Political Challenges

Analysis of the 2010 and 2014 Midterm Elections and Their Impact on Obama's Agenda

The midterm elections of 2010 and 2014 proved to be pivotal moments in Barack Obama's presidency, with significant implications for his policy agenda and the balance of power in Washington. Both elections saw significant gains for the Republican Party, as voters expressed frustration with the direction of the country and handed control of the House of Representatives and later the Senate to Republicans. The shift in power led to increased gridlock and partisan polarization in Washington, making it difficult for Obama to advance his legislative priorities and prompting him to rely more heavily on executive action to achieve his policy goals.

The 2010 Midterm Elections

The 2010 midterm elections were a major setback for the Democratic Party and the Obama administration, as Republicans capitalized on voter dissatisfaction with the struggling economy and the passage of the Affordable Care Act to gain control of the House of Representatives. Republicans picked up 63 seats in the House, giving them a majority for the first time since 2006, and significantly reducing the Democratic majority in the Senate.

The Republican takeover of the House had profound implications for Obama's legislative agenda, as it effectively put an end to any hopes of passing major initiatives through Congress. With Republicans in control of the House, Obama faced staunch opposition to his policy proposals, including efforts to stimulate the economy, reform healthcare, and address climate change. The gridlock and partisan polarization that ensued made it difficult for Obama to make progress on his legislative priorities, forcing him to rely more heavily on executive action to achieve his policy goals.

One of the most significant consequences of the 2010 midterm elections was the impact on healthcare reform. With Republicans in control of the House, efforts to repeal or undermine the Affordable Care Act intensified, leading to numerous attempts to defund or dismantle the law. While Republicans were unsuccessful in their efforts to repeal the law outright, they were able to chip away at certain provisions and hinder its implementation, leading to ongoing uncertainty and instability in the healthcare system.

The 2014 Midterm Elections

The 2014 midterm elections continued the trend of Republican gains, as the party expanded its majority in the House and regained control of the Senate for the first time since 2006. Republicans picked up nine seats in the Senate, giving them a majority of 54 seats, and further solidifying their control of Congress.

The Republican victories in the 2014 midterm elections were largely attributed to dissatisfaction with the Obama administration and its handling of a range of issues, including the economy, healthcare, and national security. The results were seen as a repudiation of Obama's policies and a sign of the public's desire for change.

The shift in power in Washington had significant implications for Obama's agenda in his final two years in office. With Republicans in control of both chambers of Congress, Obama faced even greater obstacles to advancing his policy priorities, as Republicans vowed to block his agenda at every turn. The gridlock and partisan polarization that characterized Obama's second term made it difficult for him to make progress on key issues, leading to frustration and disillusionment among Democrats and progressives.

Gridlock and Partisan Politics in Washington

The gridlock and partisan politics that characterized Obama's presidency were the result of a combination of factors, including ideological polarization, political polarization, and institutional barriers to cooperation. The deep ideological divisions between Democrats and Republicans made it difficult to find common ground on key issues, while the increasingly partisan nature of politics made compromise and cooperation more difficult than ever.

One of the main obstacles to cooperation in Washington was the rise of the Tea Party movement within the Republican Party. The Tea Party, which emerged in response to Obama's election and his agenda of healthcare reform and stimulus spending, advocated for a more conservative and uncompromising approach to governance, and pushed the Republican Party further to the right. The rise of the Tea Party led to increased polarization and gridlock in Congress, as Republicans became more ideologically rigid and less willing to compromise with Democrats.

Another factor contributing to gridlock and partisan politics in Washington was the increasing use of filibusters and other procedural tactics to block legislation and nominations. In the Senate, the filibuster became a routine tool of obstruction, with both parties using it to prevent the other from advancing its agenda. The abuse of procedural tactics like the filibuster made it difficult for Congress to function effectively and exacerbated partisan tensions.

The polarization and gridlock in Washington had profound implications for governance and policymaking, as it made it difficult for Congress to address pressing issues and respond to the needs of the American people. With Republicans and Democrats at loggerheads and little prospect of compromise, many important issues – including immigration reform, gun control, and climate change – remained unresolved, leaving millions of Americans frustrated and disillusioned with the political process.

In conclusion, the 2010 and 2014 midterm elections were watershed moments in Barack Obama's presidency, with significant implications for his policy agenda and the balance of power in Washington. The Republican gains in both elections led to increased gridlock and partisan polarization in Congress, making it difficult for Obama to advance his legislative priorities and prompting him to rely more heavily on executive action to achieve his policy goals. The gridlock and partisan politics that characterized Obama's presidency had profound implications for governance and policymaking, as it made it difficult for Congress to address pressing issues and respond to the needs of the American people. Despite Obama's efforts to bridge the partisan divide and find common ground, the deep ideological divisions and entrenched interests in Washington made cooperation and compromise increasingly difficult, leaving many Americans frustrated and disillusioned with the political process.

Chapter 12: Second Term and Legacy Building

Barack Obama's reelection in 2012 marked the beginning of his second term in office and presented him with an opportunity to build on the accomplishments of his first term and secure his legacy as one of the most consequential presidents in American history. With a fresh mandate from the American people and the promise of four more years in the White House, Obama set out to tackle a range of pressing issues facing the nation and to leave behind a lasting imprint on the country and the world.

Obama's Reelection in 2012 and Priorities for His Second Term

The 2012 presidential election was a hard-fought battle between Barack Obama, the incumbent Democratic president, and Mitt Romney, the Republican challenger. Despite a sluggish economic recovery and intense opposition from Republicans, Obama was able to secure reelection with a decisive victory in the Electoral College, winning 332 electoral votes to Romney's 206. Obama's victory was fueled by a diverse coalition of supporters, including young people, minorities, women, and urban voters, who turned out in large numbers to support his candidacy.

With his reelection secured, Obama wasted no time in laying out his priorities for his second term in office. In his second inaugural address in January 2013, Obama outlined an ambitious agenda focused on building a stronger and more inclusive economy, expanding access to healthcare, combating climate change, reforming immigration, and promoting equality and opportunity for all Americans. He spoke of the need to address the challenges of our time – from income inequality and climate change to gun violence and immigration reform – and called on

Americans to come together to build a better future for themselves and their children.

One of the central pillars of Obama's second-term agenda was healthcare reform, which had been a major focus of his first term in office. With the Affordable Care Act (ACA) now law, Obama sought to implement and defend the landmark healthcare reform law, despite continued opposition and attempts by Republicans to repeal or undermine it. He also prioritized efforts to strengthen and expand the law, including expanding Medicaid coverage to millions of low-income Americans and implementing key provisions like the individual mandate and insurance marketplaces.

In addition to healthcare reform, Obama also focused on other domestic policy priorities during his second term, including efforts to address income inequality, reform the criminal justice system, and promote renewable energy and environmental sustainability. He sought to build on the progress made in his first term and to lay the groundwork for a more prosperous, equitable, and sustainable future for all Americans.

Key Achievements and Challenges During His Final Years in Office

Obama's second term in office was marked by a mix of achievements and challenges, as he sought to navigate a divided Congress and a polarized political landscape while continuing to advance his policy agenda and secure his legacy as president. Despite facing fierce opposition from Republicans and enduring numerous setbacks and obstacles, Obama was able to achieve significant progress on a range of issues during his final years in office.

One of the most significant achievements of Obama's second term was the continued implementation of the Affordable Care Act, which expanded access to healthcare for millions of Americans and brought about historic reductions in the uninsured rate. Despite repeated attempts by Republicans to repeal or undermine the law, Obama was able to defend and strengthen it, ensuring that millions of Americans were able to access affordable, quality healthcare coverage.

Another major achievement of Obama's second term was the passage of comprehensive immigration reform legislation in the Senate in 2013. The bipartisan bill, which was championed by a group of senators known as the "Gang of Eight," sought to provide a path to citizenship for millions of undocumented immigrants living in the United States, strengthen border security, and reform the legal immigration system. While the bill ultimately stalled in the House of Representatives amid opposition from conservative Republicans, its passage in the Senate marked a significant step forward in the decades-long effort to reform the nation's immigration laws.

In addition to healthcare reform and immigration reform, Obama also achieved progress on other domestic policy priorities during his second term, including efforts to combat climate change, reform the criminal justice system, and promote equality and opportunity for all Americans. He took executive action to address climate change, including implementing the Clean Power Plan to reduce carbon emissions from power plants and signing the Paris Agreement to combat global warming. He also took steps to reform the criminal justice system, including commuting the sentences of hundreds of nonviolent drug offenders and advocating for sentencing reform legislation.

Despite these achievements, however, Obama's second term was not without its challenges and setbacks. The continued gridlock and partisan polarization in Washington made it difficult for him to advance his legislative agenda, leading to frustration and disillusionment among Democrats and progressives. The rise of the Tea Party within the Republican Party further exacerbated partisan tensions and hindered efforts to find common ground on key issues.

In conclusion, Barack Obama's second term in office was marked by a mix of achievements and challenges, as he sought to navigate a divided Congress and a polarized political landscape while continuing to advance his policy agenda and secure his legacy as president. Despite facing fierce opposition from Republicans and enduring numerous setbacks and obstacles, Obama was able to achieve significant progress on a range of issues during his final years in office, including healthcare reform, immigration reform, and efforts to combat climate change and reform the criminal justice system. And while much work remains to be done to address the pressing challenges facing the nation, Obama's legacy as a champion of progress, equality, and opportunity will endure as a beacon of hope and inspiration for future generations.

Chapter 13: Legacy and Impact

Assessing Barack Obama's Legacy: Successes, Shortcomings, and Lasting Impact on American Politics and Society

Barack Obama's presidency was historic in many respects, as the first African American to hold the highest office in the land. Throughout his two terms in office, Obama faced a wide range of challenges and opportunities, and his presidency left a lasting imprint on American politics and society. Assessing Obama's legacy requires examining his successes and shortcomings, as well as his impact on key issues and the public's perception of his presidency.

Successes of the Obama Presidency

One of the most significant successes of the Obama presidency was the passage of the Affordable Care Act (ACA), also known as Obamacare. Signed into law in 2010, the ACA expanded access to healthcare for millions of Americans, provided protections for individuals with pre-existing conditions, and allowed young adults to stay on their parents' insurance plans until the age of 26. The ACA also helped to reduce the uninsured rate to historic lows and brought about important reforms to the healthcare system.

Another major success of the Obama presidency was the economic recovery following the Great Recession. When Obama took office in 2009, the country was facing the worst economic downturn since the Great Depression, with millions of Americans losing their jobs and homes. Through a combination of fiscal stimulus, monetary policy, and financial regulation, Obama's administration was able to stabilize the economy and lay the groundwork for a sustained period of economic growth and job creation.

In addition to healthcare reform and economic recovery, Obama achieved progress on a range of other domestic policy priorities during his presidency. He signed into law the Dodd-Frank Wall Street Reform and Consumer Protection Act, which aimed to prevent another financial crisis by regulating the banking and financial industry. He also took executive action to address climate change, including implementing the Clean Power Plan to reduce carbon emissions from power plants and signing the Paris Agreement to combat global warming.

Obama's presidency was also marked by significant progress on social issues, including LGBTQ rights and criminal justice reform. He repealed the military's discriminatory "Don't Ask, Don't Tell" policy, allowing gay and lesbian service members to serve openly in the military. He also commuted the sentences of hundreds of nonviolent drug offenders and advocated for sentencing reform legislation to address disparities in the criminal justice system.

Shortcomings of the Obama Presidency

Despite his successes, Barack Obama's presidency was not without its shortcomings. One of the most notable shortcomings was the failure to achieve comprehensive immigration reform. Despite repeated attempts to pass legislation to provide a path to citizenship for undocumented immigrants, Obama was unable to overcome opposition from Republicans in Congress, leading to ongoing uncertainty and instability in the immigration system.

Another major shortcoming of the Obama presidency was the inability to bridge the partisan divide and overcome gridlock in Washington. Despite his efforts to reach across the aisle and find common ground with Republicans, Obama faced staunch opposition from conservative lawmakers who were unwilling to compromise on key issues. This gridlock and polarization made it difficult for Obama to advance his legislative agenda and address pressing challenges facing the nation.

Obama's foreign policy also faced criticism, particularly in the Middle East. Critics argued that Obama's policies, including the withdrawal of troops from Iraq and the decision not to intervene more forcefully in the Syrian civil war, contributed to instability in the region and allowed terrorist groups like ISIS to gain strength. Obama's handling of conflicts in Libya and Yemen also drew criticism for lacking a clear strategy and leading to unintended consequences.

In addition to these shortcomings, Obama's presidency was also marked by challenges and setbacks on issues like gun control and racial inequality. Despite repeated calls for action in the wake of mass shootings, Obama was unable to pass meaningful gun control legislation due to opposition from Republicans and the powerful gun lobby. And while Obama spoke out against racial inequality and police brutality, his administration faced criticism for not doing enough to address systemic racism and injustice.

Lasting Impact on American Politics and Society

Despite its shortcomings, Barack Obama's presidency had a lasting impact on American politics and society. Obama's election in 2008 shattered barriers and inspired millions of Americans, particularly people of color, to believe that anything was possible. His presidency brought a sense of hope and optimism to the country, and his message of unity and inclusion resonated with people from all walks of life.

Obama's presidency also helped to redefine the role of government and the expectations of what government can and should do. Through initiatives like the ACA and economic stimulus package, Obama demonstrated the power of government to improve people's lives and address pressing challenges facing the nation. He also challenged conventional wisdom on issues like healthcare and climate change, pushing for bold and ambitious solutions to complex problems.

In addition to his policy accomplishments, Obama's presidency also had a profound impact on American culture and society. His embrace of social media and use of technology helped to revolutionize political communication and engagement, mobilizing millions of young people and energizing a new generation of activists. His advocacy for LGBTQ rights and criminal justice reform helped to change hearts and minds and advance the cause of equality and justice for all Americans.

Public Perception of Obama's Presidency and His Place in History

Barack Obama's presidency elicited a wide range of opinions and emotions from the American people, and his legacy remains a subject of debate and discussion. While many Americans view Obama as a transformative figure who brought about positive change and progress, others criticize his policies and leadership style and question his impact on the country.

According to public opinion polls, Obama left office with relatively high approval ratings, with a majority of Americans expressing support for his handling of key issues like healthcare and the economy. However, his presidency also faced criticism from both the left and the right, with progressives faulting him for not being bold enough in pursuing their agenda and conservatives accusing him of overreach and incompetence.

In terms of his place in history, Barack Obama is likely to be remembered as one of the most consequential presidents of the modern era. His election in 2008 represented a historic milestone in American history and signaled a profound shift in the country's political landscape. His presidency brought about significant changes in policy and politics, and his legacy continues to shape the direction of the country and the world.

In conclusion, Barack Obama's presidency was marked by successes and shortcomings, achievements and challenges. His presidency brought about significant changes in American politics and society, and his legacy continues to be debated and discussed by historians, scholars, and the American people. While Obama's presidency may not have been perfect, his impact on the country and the world is undeniable, and his legacy as a transformative figure in American history is likely to endure for generations to come.

Chapter 14: Post-Presidency

Barack Obama's life after leaving the Oval Office in January 2017 has been marked by a combination of activism, writing, and the establishment of the Obama Foundation. As the first African American president of the United States, Obama's post-presidential activities have continued to shape the political landscape and inspire millions of people around the world. This chapter will delve into Obama's post-presidency endeavors, examining his activism, writing projects, and the impact of the Obama Foundation on the current political landscape.

Activism: Continuing the Fight for Change

Since leaving office, Barack Obama has remained actively engaged in political and social issues, using his platform to advocate for causes close to his heart. One of the key areas of focus for Obama has been voting rights and democracy reform. He has spoken out against efforts to restrict voting access, particularly targeting voter suppression laws that disproportionately affect minority communities. Obama has called for measures to expand access to voting, including automatic voter registration and making Election Day a national holiday.

In addition to voting rights, Obama has also been vocal on issues such as healthcare, climate change, and immigration reform. He has criticized efforts to dismantle the Affordable Care Act and has called for action to address the urgent threat of climate change. Obama has also spoken out against the Trump administration's immigration policies, including the separation of families at the border and the travel ban targeting predominantly Muslim countries.

In his post-presidency, Obama has continued to emphasize the importance of civic engagement and grassroots activism. He has encouraged young people to get involved in their communities and participate in the political process, often citing his own experiences as a community organizer in Chicago. Obama has also expressed optimism about the future of the country, urging Americans to remain hopeful and engaged in the fight for progress and change.

Writing Projects: Reflecting on Leadership and Legacy

In addition to his activism, Barack Obama has also devoted time to writing, penning a memoir reflecting on his presidency and his life in public service. Titled "A Promised Land," the memoir was published in November 2020 and quickly became a bestseller, offering readers an intimate glimpse into Obama's time in office and the challenges he faced as president.

In "A Promised Land," Obama reflects on his early years in politics, his historic election as the first African American president, and his efforts to navigate the complexities of governing in a deeply divided country. He offers candid insights into his decision-making process, the highs and lows of his presidency, and the enduring lessons he learned along the way. The memoir provides a behind-the-scenes look at Obama's presidency, offering readers a deeper understanding of the man and his leadership style.

In addition to his memoir, Obama has also written essays and op-eds on a range of topics, including democracy, race relations, and the future of the country. He has used his writing to weigh in on current events and offer his perspective on issues facing the nation, often drawing on his own experiences as president.

The Obama Foundation: Building a Legacy of Leadership

Central to Barack Obama's post-presidential activities has been the establishment of the Obama Foundation, a nonprofit organization dedicated to inspiring and empowering the next generation of leaders. The foundation was founded in 2014 with the goal of fostering civic engagement, promoting leadership development, and addressing some of the most pressing challenges facing communities around the world.

Through initiatives like the Obama Presidential Center in Chicago, the foundation seeks to create a space for dialogue, collaboration, and innovation, where people from diverse backgrounds can come together to exchange ideas and work towards positive change. The center will include a museum, library, and community center, as well as programming and events focused on leadership development, civic engagement, and community organizing.

In addition to the Obama Presidential Center, the foundation also runs a number of programs and initiatives aimed at empowering young people to make a difference in their communities. These include the Obama Scholars Program, which provides scholarships and leadership training to promising young leaders from around the world, and the Obama Fellowship, which supports individuals working on innovative projects to address social and environmental challenges.

The Obama Foundation has also launched initiatives focused on issues like criminal justice reform, climate change, and economic opportunity, working in partnership with local organizations and communities to drive meaningful change. Through its programming and outreach efforts, the foundation seeks to build on the legacy of Barack Obama's presidency and inspire a new generation of leaders to take action and make a difference in the world.

Impact on the Current Political Landscape

Barack Obama's post-presidential activities have had a significant impact on the current political landscape, shaping the conversation around key issues and inspiring a new generation of leaders to get involved in the political process. His advocacy on issues like voting rights, healthcare, and climate change has helped to mobilize grassroots activists and elevate these issues on the national agenda.

In addition, Obama's memoir and writing projects have provided valuable insights into his presidency and leadership style, offering readers a deeper understanding of the challenges he faced and the decisions he made while in office. By sharing his experiences and reflecting on his time in the White House, Obama has helped to shape the narrative around his presidency and his place in history.

The Obama Foundation, meanwhile, has become a hub for leadership development and civic engagement, providing resources and support to young people who are passionate about making a difference in their communities. Through its programs and initiatives, the foundation is helping to cultivate the next generation of leaders and empower them to tackle some of the most pressing challenges facing society.

In conclusion, Barack Obama's post-presidency has been characterized by activism, writing, and the establishment of the Obama Foundation. Through his advocacy, writing projects, and foundation work, Obama continues to make a meaningful impact on the political landscape and inspire millions of people around the world to get involved in the fight for progress and change. As he continues his work in the years ahead, Obama's legacy as a transformative leader and champion of hope and change will endure, shaping the future of the country and the world for generations to come.

Chapter 15: Conclusion

Reflecting on the Enduring Legacy of the Obama Presidency and Its Significance in the 21st Century

The Obama presidency stands as a pivotal chapter in American history, marked by hope, change, and progress. From his historic election as the nation's first African American president to his ambitious agenda to address pressing challenges at home and abroad, Barack Obama's tenure in office left an indelible imprint on the country and the world. As we reflect on the legacy of the Obama presidency and its significance in the 21st century, it is clear that his leadership and vision continue to shape the course of American politics and society.

One of the most enduring legacies of the Obama presidency is his commitment to inclusivity and diversity. Throughout his time in office, Obama sought to bridge the racial and cultural divides that have long plagued American society, emphasizing the importance of unity and empathy in the face of adversity. By breaking down barriers and challenging stereotypes, Obama inspired millions of people, particularly people of color, to believe that anything was possible, regardless of their background or circumstances.

Another key aspect of the Obama presidency was its focus on progressive policy priorities, including healthcare reform, climate change, and social justice. Through initiatives like the Affordable Care Act, the Clean Power Plan, and criminal justice reform, Obama sought to address some of the most pressing challenges facing the nation and leave behind a more equitable and sustainable future for all Americans. While progress on these issues was often slow and incremental, Obama's presidency laid the groundwork for future reform efforts and inspired a new generation of activists and leaders to continue the fight for change.

In addition to his policy accomplishments, Barack Obama's presidency was also marked by his leadership on the world stage. From his efforts to reset relations with Russia to his engagement with Iran and Cuba, Obama sought to promote diplomacy and cooperation as a means of addressing global challenges and advancing America's interests. While his approach to foreign policy was not without its critics, Obama's commitment to multilateralism and engagement helped to restore America's standing in the world and fostered greater collaboration on issues like climate change and nuclear nonproliferation.

Lessons Learned and Implications for Future Leaders

As we look back on the Obama presidency and its lasting impact, there are several important lessons to be learned and implications for future leaders. One lesson is the importance of perseverance and resilience in the face of adversity. Throughout his time in office, Obama faced intense opposition and criticism from political opponents, but he never wavered in his commitment to his principles and vision for the country. His ability to stay focused and determined in the face of challenges serves as a powerful example for future leaders who may encounter similar obstacles.

Another lesson of the Obama presidency is the importance of empathy and understanding in leadership. Obama's ability to connect with people from all walks of life, to listen to their concerns, and to empathize with their struggles, helped to bridge divides and build consensus around key issues. In an era of increasing polarization and division, the need for leaders who can bring people together and find common ground has never been greater.

Additionally, the Obama presidency underscored the importance of integrity and honesty in leadership. Throughout his time in office, Obama was known for his integrity and moral compass, even in the face of difficult decisions and political pressure. His commitment to transparency and accountability helped to restore trust in government and set a high standard for future leaders to follow.

Looking ahead, the legacy of the Obama presidency will continue to shape the trajectory of American politics and society for years to come. As future leaders grapple with the challenges of the 21st century, they would do well to heed the lessons of Obama's presidency – to embrace inclusivity and diversity, to persevere in the face of adversity, to lead with empathy and integrity, and to work tirelessly to build a more just, equitable, and sustainable future for all. In doing so, they will honor the legacy of Barack Obama and ensure that his vision of hope and change endures for generations to come.

Don't miss out!

Visit the website below and you can sign up to receive emails whenever Michael Johnson publishes a new book. There's no charge and no obligation.

https://books2read.com/r/B-A-OREFB-CSXAD

BOOKS 2 READ

Connecting independent readers to independent writers.

Did you love *The Obama Presidency*? Then you should read *Founding Fathers*[1] by Michael Johnson!

[2]

"Founding Fathers: The Birth of a Nation" offers a captivating journey through the genesis of the United States. From the seeds of dissent to the forging of alliances, delve into the pivotal moments and key figures that shaped America's birth. Explore the drafting of the Declaration of Independence, the trials of the Revolutionary War, and the crafting of the Constitution. Reflect on the enduring legacy of the Founding Fathers and their vision for a nation founded on principles of liberty and democracy. This comprehensive account illuminates the evolution of the American experiment and its ongoing pursuit of freedom and equality."

---

1. https://books2read.com/u/49arJY

2. https://books2read.com/u/49arJY

About the Author

Michael Johnson is a distinguished historian specializing in American history. With a degree in History from Harvard University, Johnson's work delves into pivotal moments, figures, and themes shaping the United States. He has authored numerous acclaimed books, offering insightful perspectives and engaging narratives. Johnson's commitment to meticulous scholarship and compelling storytelling has earned him widespread acclaim in the field. Passionate about sharing his expertise, he frequently engages in lectures and public events to foster a deeper appreciation for America's past.